World Series Champions: Los Angeles Angels

First baseman Rod Carew

Pitcher Francisco Rodríguez

WORLD SERIES CHAMPIONS

LOS ANGELES ANGELS

MICHAEL E. GOODMAN

CREATIVE EDUCATION / CREATIVE PAPERBACKS

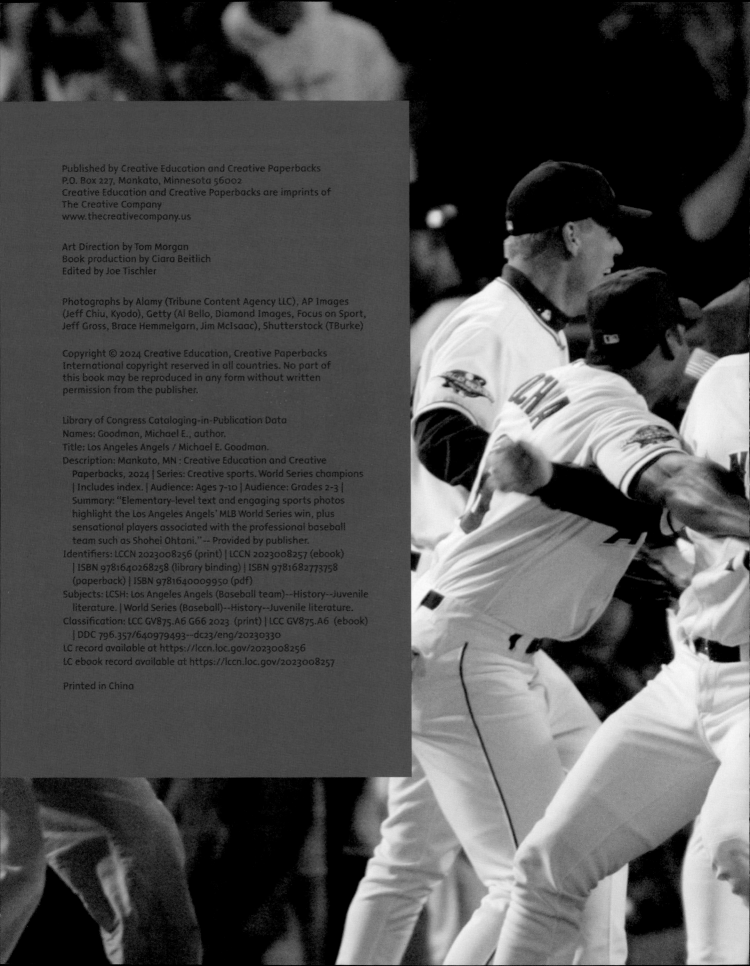

Published by Creative Education and Creative Paperbacks
P.O. Box 227, Mankato, Minnesota 56002
Creative Education and Creative Paperbacks are imprints of
The Creative Company
www.thecreativecompany.us

Art Direction by Tom Morgan
Book production by Ciara Beitlich
Edited by Joe Tischler

Photographs by Alamy (Tribune Content Agency LLC), AP Images
(Jeff Chiu, Kyodo), Getty (Al Bello, Diamond Images, Focus on Sport,
Jeff Gross, Brace Hemmelgarn, Jim McIsaac), Shutterstock (TBurke)

Library of Congress Cataloging-in-Publication Data
Names: Goodman, Michael E., author.
Title: Los Angeles Angels / Michael E. Goodman.
Description: Mankato, MN : Creative Education and Creative
    Paperbacks, 2024 | Series: Creative sports. World Series champions
    | Includes index. | Audience: Ages 7-10 | Audience: Grades 2-3 |
    Summary: "Elementary-level text and engaging sports photos
    highlight the Los Angeles Angels' MLB World Series win, plus
    sensational players associated with the professional baseball
    team such as Shohei Ohtani." -- Provided by publisher.
Identifiers: LCCN 2023008256 (print) | LCCN 2023008257 (ebook)
    | ISBN 9781640268258 (library binding) | ISBN 9781682773758
    (paperback) | ISBN 9781640009950 (pdf)
Subjects: LCSH: Los Angeles Angels (Baseball team)--History--Juvenile
    literature. | World Series (Baseball)--History--Juvenile literature.
Classification: LCC GV875.A6 G66 2023 (print) | LCC GV875.A6 (ebook)
    | DDC 796.357/640979493--dc23/eng/20230330
LC record available at https://lccn.loc.gov/2023008256
LC ebook record available at https://lccn.loc.gov/2023008257

Printed in China

2002 World Series Champions

Outfielder Mike Trout

CONTENTS

Home of the Angels

Los Angeles (LA), California, is a sprawling city near the Pacific Ocean. Millions of people live there. Close to LA is a smaller city named Anaheim. That's where the LA Angels baseball team plays. Every year, fans pack Angel Stadium of Anaheim to cheer them on.

The Los Angeles Angels are a Major League Baseball (MLB) team. They play in the American League (AL) West Division. Their **rivals** are the Oakland Athletics. All MLB teams want to win the World Series and become champions.

Pitcher Nolan Ryan

Naming the Angels

Los Angeles is often called the "City of Angels." But that's not where the baseball team's nickname comes from. It comes from an earlier baseball team in the city also named "Angels." The full name of the club has changed several times. They are now what they started out as, the Los Angeles Angels.

Pitcher Dean Chance

Angels History

The Angels became a new team in the AL in 1961. Pitcher Dean Chance was one of the club's first stars. In 1964, he won the Cy Young Award. The award is given to the season's best pitcher. In 1972, hard-throwing pitcher Nolan Ryan joined the Angels. His blazing fastball was hard to hit. He led the AL in strikeouts seven times as an Angel.

The Angels did not make the **playoffs** until 1979. That season, sluggers Don Baylor and Bobby Grich led the way. Baylor smacked 36 home runs, and Grich added 30. The Angels made the playoffs again in 1982 and 1986. But they could not reach the World Series.

Outfielder Don Baylor

Third baseman Troy Glaus

In 2002, the Angels reached new heights. They won 99 games and earned their first AL **pennant**. Then they beat the San Francisco Giants to become World Champions! Third baseman Troy Glaus was named the series Most Valuable Player (MVP).

Manager Mike Scioscia (SOH-sha) led the Angels to the top of the AL West in the 2000s. The team finished first in its division six times. Outfielder Mike Trout is one of baseball's biggest stars. He's won three AL MVP awards.

Other Angels Stars

Rod Carew and Vladimir Guerrero were All-Stars several times as Angels. They are now in the Baseball **Hall of Fame**.

Pitcher Chuck Finley won 165 games for the Angels. That is a team record. **Closer** Francisco Rodríguez saved 62 games in 2008. No major league pitcher has done better.

Outfielder Vladimir Guerrero

Pitcher/Designated hitter Shohei Ohtani